I am going to... Spain

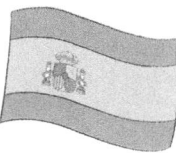

This book belongs to

Text and illustrations copyright © Nerea Kennedy 2023.

All rights reserved. No part of this publication may be reproduced, stored in a retrieval system, distributed, or transmitted in any form or by any means, including photocopying, recording, or other electronic or mechanical methods, without the prior written permission of the publisher, except in the case of brief quotations, embodied in critical reviews and certain other noncommercial uses permitted by copyright law. Moral rights asserted.

ISBN 978-1-915745-10-1

A catalogue record for this book is available from the British Library

Welcome to, I am going on holidays to ...
Spain!
A fun way to learn Spanish before you go on holidays with many cute illustrations.

Ideally suited for children aged 9 and above as they discover a new language.

How to use this book
This book is divided in two:

- **The first section of this book is full of fun activities to help you learn the Spanish you need before going to Spain or whilst on holidays.**
- **The second section has** 14 FUN tasks **to do and put speaking Spanish into practice while on holidays.**
- **Feel free to trace and colour all the images you find along the way.**
- **Once you have done a task, please tick the box provided in the page to remind you of the ones that are left to do.**

A message for the adults

- **Encourage your children to say the new words out loud, this will help them to practise speaking Spanish and help them to remember the new words discovered.**
- **Reward children with plenty of praise and encouragement.**
- **Make learning Spanish fun for you and your children**

--- Contents ---

Spanish to learn before travelling or whilst in Spain:

1. **Greetings**

2. **Essential words**

3. **Numbers**

4. **Typical Spanish drinks & food**
   Breakfast, lunch, tea and dinner.
   Fruits, desserts, ice creams and sweets

5. **Places to visit**

6. **Examples of conversations:**
   In the restaurant, the ice cream parlor and the sweet shop!!!

7. **Basic Grammar ~ recap** *It's Fun!*

8. **The best questions to ask**

Spanish cities: BEST places to visit and what to do to have an awesome time in ...

Madrid, Barcelona, Valencia, Sevilla, Málaga, Mallorca, Santiago de Compostela

14 FUN TASKS with 160 CHALLENGES
practice speaking Spanish during your holidays

♡ This is Mia,
let Mia, her family and friends teach you Spanish

Mia

Mia's friends ~ Los amigos de Mia

Noah   **Alice**   **Tom**

Oliver   **Molly**

Mia's brother ~   Mia's sister ~
El hermano de Mia   La hermana de Mia

William   **Rose**

In Spanish to say ...

 Hello ... we say .... **Hola**

 My name is ... we say ... **Me llamo**

 ♡ **Hola, me llamo Mia.**

~ Hello, my name is Mia ~

♡ Please say hello to Mia in Spanish and tell her your name

_ _ _ _ , _ _ _ _ _ _ _ _ _ _

--- Greetings ---

In Spanish to say ...

Good morning ... we say .... **Buenos días**

Good afternoon... we say ... **Buenas tardes**

Good evening ... we say .... **Buenas noches**

♡ **Buenos días, me llamo Oliver**

~ Good morning, my name is Oliver ~

♡ **Please match the correct greetings**

Buenas tardes   Good morning

Buenos días   Good afternoon

Buenas noches   Good evening

--- Greetings ---

In Spanish to say ...

 Hello   Hola

 How are you?   ¿Cómo estás?

Very well   Muy bien

 Thank you   *We say*   Gracias

See you later Hasta luego

 Goodbye   Adiós

♡ **Hola, me llamo Alice, ¿Cómo estás?**

~ Hello, my name is Alice, how are you? ~

♡ **Muy bien, gracias**

~ Very well, thank you ~

--- Greetings ---

♡ Match the English with the Spanish words

Adiós

Hello

Thank you

Muy bien

Hasta luego

Gracias

¿Cómo estás?

Very well

How are you?

Hola

See you later

Goodbye

--- Greetings ---

♡ Can you write in Spanish what the children are saying?

♡ Good morning

_____ _____

♡ Good afternoon

_____ _____

♡ Good evening

_____ _____

♡ How are you?

_____ _____

--- Essential words ---

In Spanish to say ...

♡ Yes	♡ Si
♡ No	♡ No
♡ And	♡ Y
♡ Please	♡ Por favor
♡ Thank you	♡ Gracias
♡ You are welcome	♡ De nada
♡ Big	♡ Grande
♡ Small	♡ Pequeño/a
♡ With	♡ Con
♡ Without	♡ Sin

we say

♡ Look at the words above, try to read them out loud

Essential words

♡ Please find the essential words in the word search below

Por favor ☐

Gracias ☐

De nada ☐

Si ☐

No ☐

Sin ☐

P	O	R	E	F	A	V	O	R
A	W	O	R	X	D	P	T	B
H	S	A	I	C	A	R	G	I
Y	I	Q	S	U	N	O	A	N
U	N	I	J	K	Q	U	L	M
V	I	D	F	A	E	L	C	O
S	E	O	G	B	D	U	T	N

♡ Can you write in English what the children are saying?

♡ Muchas gracias

- - - - - - - - -   - - - - - - - - -

♡ De nada

- - - - -   - - - - -   - - - - -

--- Essential words ---

♡ Can you guess what are they saying?

♡ Gracias

- - - - - - - - - - - -

♡ Por favor

- - - - - - - - - - -

♡ De nada

- - - - - - -   - - - - -   - - - - - - - - - -

♡ Grande

- - - - - - - - - - -

♡ Pequeño

- - - - - - - - - - -

--- Essential words ---

♡ Match the English with the Spanish words

♡ Sin
♡ Yes
♡ Please
♡ Con
♡ You are welcome
♡ Por favor
♡ Thank you
♡ Small
♡ With
♡ Grande
♡ Si
♡ Without
♡ No
♡ De nada
♡ Big
♡ Pequeño
♡ No
♡ Gracias

--- Numbers ---

♡ Colour the numbers

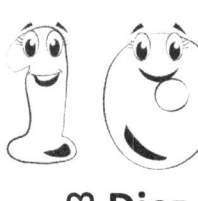
♡ Diez

♡ Uno

♡ Dos

♡ Nueve

♡ Tres

♡ Ocho

♡ Cuatro

♡ Siete

♡ Seis

♡ Cinco

--- Numbers ---

♡ Copy the numbers in Spanish

♡ Cero

♡ Uno

♡ Dos

♡ Tres

♡ Cuatro

♡ Cinco

--- Numbers ---

♡ **Copy the numbers in Spanish**

♡ **Seis**

♡ **Siete**

♡ **Ocho**

♡ **Nueve**

♡ **Diez**

--- Numbers ---

♡ Trace and name the numbers in Spanish

--- Typical Spanish: drinks

♡ Spanish Children's favorite drinks!!!

In Spanish to say ...

we say

♡ Water	♡ Agua
♡ Sparkling water	♡ Agua con gas
♡ Mineral water	♡ Agua sin gas
♡ Milk	♡ Leche
♡ Milkshake	♡ Batido de Leche
♡ Orange juice	♡ Zumo de naranja
♡ Peach juice	♡ Zumo de melocotón
♡ Lemonade	♡ Limonada
♡ With ice	♡ Con hielo
♡ Without ice	♡ Sin hielo
♡ Cold	♡ Fria/o

--- Typical Spanish: drinks

♡ Match the Spanish drinks with their English names

♡ Leche

♡ Agua sin gas

♡ Zumo de naranja

♡ Batido de fresa

♡ Limonada sin hielo

♡ Mineral water
♡ Milk
♡ Orange juice
♡ Strawberry milkshake
♡ Lemonade
♡ Without ice

--- Typical Spanish: drinks

In Spanish to say ...

~ A bottle ~
♡ **Una botella**

~ A glass ~
♡ **Un vaso**

we say

♡ **Hola, una botella de agua por favor**

~ Hello, a bottle of water please ~

♡ **Write what the children need in English**

♡ **Hola, un vaso de leche por favor**

♡ **Hola, un vaso de limonada por favor**

--- Typical Spanish: drinks

In Spanish to say ...

  I want ... we say .... **Quiero**

♡ **Hola, quiero un zumo de naranja por favor**

~ Hello, I want an orange juice please ~

It's **NOT** rude to use "I want", that's the way we say it!

♡ **Please find the drinks in the word search below**

A	L	A	I	X	Z	U	M	O
G	G	J	N	O	M	B	I	Y
U	S	N	U	L	W	O	Z	P
A	Q	A	T	E	E	D	F	U
O	D	R	O	I	S	C	J	A
I	R	A	A	H	L	Y	H	W
Y	E	N	I	O	U	I	A	E

Naranja ☐

Leche ☐

Zumo ☐

Agua ☐

Hielo ☐

--- Typical Spanish: food

♡ **Breakfast ~ Desayuno**

In Spanish to say ... *we say*

♡ Cereals	♡ Cereales
♡ Toast	♡ Tostada
♡ Butter	♡ Mantequilla
♡ Marmalade	♡ Mermelada
♡ Tomato	♡ Tomate
♡ Bacon	♡ Panceta
♡ Fried eggs	♡ Huevos fritos
♡ Churros	♡ Churros
♡ Yogurt	♡ Yogur
♡ Fruit	♡ Fruta

--- Typical Spanish: food

--- Typical Spanish: food

♡ "a", "an" and "some"

In Spanish all nouns are defined as masculine or feminine, there are different genders!
We also have to be careful if we are talking about one thing or more than one!

Let's talk about toast and tomatoes

♡ "toast" has a feminine gender:

"a" toast ⟹ "UNA" tostada

"some" toast ⟹ "UNAS" tostadas

♡ Una Tostada   ♡ Unas Tostadas

♡ "tomato" has a masculine gender:

"a" tomato ⟹ "UN" tomate

"some" tomatoes ⟹ "UNOS" tomate

♡ Un Tomate   ♡ Unos Tomates

--- Typical Spanish: food

♡ Draw a picture of the following items

♡ **Una Tostada**

♡ **Un Tomate**

♡ **Una fruta**

♡ **Un Yogur**

♡ **Unos Huevos fritos**

♡ Remember

♡ "a" & "an" = "un" or "una"
♡ "some" = "unos" or "unas"

--- Typical Spanish: food

♡ **Breakfast ~ Desayuno**

Spanish children's favorite breakfast!!!

♡ Churros con/sin chocolate	♡ A pastry similar to a doughnut, fried in hot oil and coated in cinnamon and sugar... yummy! They are normally served with hot dark chocolate
♡ Pan con tomate	♡ A toast with tomato, a little bit of garlic and olive oil on top, strangely nice and very healthy!
♡ Galletas Maria	♡ A plain but sweet biscuit with a hint of vanilla, similar to the "Rich tea" biscuits in the UK

--- Typical Spanish: food

♡ Can you write in English what the children are saying?

♡ Buenos días, un vaso de leche y unas galletas Maria por favor.

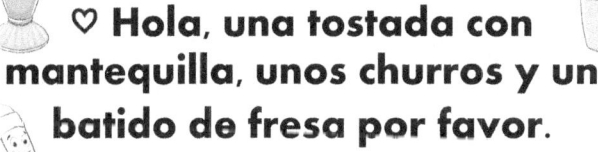

♡ Hola, una tostada con mantequilla, unos churros y un batido de fresa por favor.

♡ Quiero pan con tomate, unos huevos fritos y panceta, gracias.

--- Typical Spanish: food

♡ "Hay"

In Spanish the word "hay" means "there is" OR "there are"

"there **is**" fruit → "**Hay**" fruta

"there **are**" cereals "**Hay**" cereales

Let's talk about eggs and yogurts!

♡ <u>¿Hay huevos?</u> ~ Are there eggs? ~

♡ **Si, hay dos huevos**
~ Yes, there are 2 eggs ~

♡ **No, no hay huevos**
~ No, there are no eggs ~

?

♡ Finish the answers in <u>Spanish</u>

♡ <u>¿Hay yogures?</u> ~ Are there yogurts? ~

♡ Si, ¬ _ _ _ _ _ _ _ _ _ _ _ _ _

♡ Si, hay ¬ _ _ _ _ _ _ _ _ _ _ _

--- Typical Spanish: food

♡ What is in each of the bubbles?
Draw pictures of the named items

♡ Hay un yogurt

♡ Hay mantequilla

♡ Hay churros

♡ Hay pan con tomate

♡ Hay panceta

♡ Remember

♡ "hay" = "there is" or "there are"

--- Typical Spanish: food

♡ Can you write in <u>Spanish</u> what the children are saying?

♡ **Good afternoon, Is there peach juice? I want a peach juice and 2 toasts with butter please**

♡ Please find the food in the word search below

	T	Z	E	T	U	D	I	E	Z
Tapas ☐	U	A	L	L	I	T	R	O	T
Paella ☐	E	T	O	X	M	S	E	N	U
Tortilla ☐	V	U	Z	P	A	O	H	I	J
Tostada ☐	O	R	I	P	A	E	L	L	A
Fruta ☐	E	F	A	U	F	S	U	X	O
	B	T	O	S	T	A	D	A	E

--- Typical Spanish: food

> ♡ **Lunch & dinner ~ Comida y cena**

Spanish children's favorite meals!!!

♡ Tapas	♡ Little plates of Spanish style appetizers... yummy!
♡ Paella	♡ A rice dish that can be made with chicken or sea food
♡ Ensalada rusa	♡ A diced potato and vegetable salad with mayonnaise
♡ Tortilla Española	♡ A potato omelet with or without onion
♡ Croquetas	♡ Croquettes can be made with lots of different ingredients. Spanish children LOVE them with chicken or ham !!!

--- Typical Spanish: food

 **In Spanish to say ...**

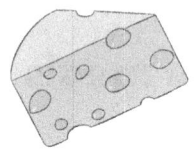 ~ A portion ~ *we say*
♡ **Una ración**

♡ **Buenas tardes, una ración de paella por favor**

~ Good afternoon, a portion of paella please ~

♡ **Write what the children need in English**

♡ **Hola, una ración de ensalada rusa por favor**

- -

♡ **Buenos días, una ración de croquetas por favor**

- -

--- Typical Spanish: food

♡ Can you write in **English** what the children are saying?

♡ **Buenos días, quiero una botella de agua por favor**

♡ **Buenas tardes, una ración de paella y agua sin gas con hielo por favor**

♡ **Hola, quiero un zumo de naranja y una ración de tortilla de patata sin cebolla.**

--- Typical Spanish: food

♡ **Lunch & dinner ~ Comida y cena**

In Spanish to say ...   *we say*

♡ Chicken	♡ Pollo
♡ Calamari	♡ Calamares
♡ Prawns	♡ Gambas
♡ Sea food	♡ Marisco
♡ Serrano ham	♡ Jamón serrano
♡ Ham	♡ Jamón
♡ Loin fillet	♡ Lomo
♡ Fried eggs	♡ Huevos fritos

♡ How many chicken pieces, calamari and fried eggs are there? (Answer in Spanish)

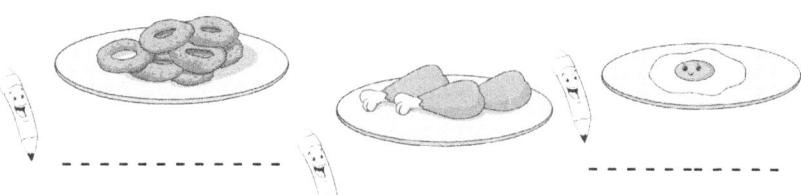

--- Typical Spanish: food

♡ Match the Spanish food with the English ones

♡ **Huevos fritos**

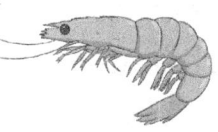

♡ **Gambas**

♡ Loin fillet
♡ Chicken
♡ Calamari
♡ Fried eggs
♡ Prawns

♡ **Calamares**

♡ **Lomo**

♡ **Polllo**

--- Typical Spanish: food

♡ La merienda ~ Tea / Afternoon snack

In Spain "la merienda" consist ALWAYS of a "bocadillo" or a "sandwich" of nutella, ham, cheese, serrano ham or chorizo with a piece of fruit and a drink.

Spanish children's favorite meal!!!

♡ Bocadillo	♡ A sandwich made with a French baguette, called "pan" / bread ... yummy!
♡ Sandwich	♡ A sandwich made with sliced bread, the same used for toast.
♡ Relleno: Nutella, jamón, queso, jamón serrano y chorizo	♡ Fillings: Nutella, ham, cheese, serrano ham and chorizo... the choice is endless!!!
♡ Fruta & Bebida	♡ Fruit & drink

♡ Bocadillo   ♡ Fruta

♡ Sandwich

♡ Bebida

--- Typical Spanish: food

> ♡ La merienda ~
> Tea / Afternoon snack

♡ Buenos tardes, un bocadillo de jamòn y una botella de agua por favor.

Noah

♡ Hola, quiero un sandwich de chorizo y queso y un batido de fresa por favor.

Alice

♡ Quiero un sandwich de Nutella y un zumo de naranja.

Oliver

♡ Buenos tardes, un bocadillo de jamòn serrano y un vaso de agua con hielo por favor.

Molly

> ♡ Who is ordering what? Can you match the order with the name?

1 ♡ A serrano ham sandwich and a glass of water with ice.   *Alice*

2 ♡ A Nutella sandwich and an orange juice.   *Molly*

3 ♡ A ham sandwich and a bottle of water.   *Noah*

4 ♡ A chorizo and cheese sandwich and a strawberry milkshake.   *Oliver*

--- Typical Spanish: food

♡ Desert - (Fruit) ~ Postre – (Fruta)

♡ Orange	♡ Naranja
♡ Apple	♡ Manzana
♡ Banana	♡ Plátano
♡ Strawberries	♡ Fresas
♡ Pineapple	♡ Piña
♡ Watermelon	♡ Sandia
♡ Cherries	♡ Cerezas
♡ Lemon	♡ Limòn
♡ Grapes	♡ Uvas
♡ Pear	♡ Pera

♡ Write what she wants in <u>English</u>

♡ Quiero fresas por favor

- -

--- Typical Spanish: food

♡ Colour the fruits

♡ Piña
♡ limón
♡ Naranja
♡ cerezas
♡ Pera
♡ Piña
♡ Uvas
♡ Manzana
♡ Plátano
♡ Sandia

--- Typical Spanish: food

> ♡ "The"

In Spanish, all nouns are defined as masculine or feminine, there are different genders!
We also have to be careful if we are talking about one thing or more than one!

Let's talk about oranges and lemons!

♡ "orange" has a feminine gender:

"the" orange ⟹ "LA" naranja

"the" oranges ⟹ "LAS" naranjas

♡ **La naranja**   ♡ **Las naranjas**

♡ "lemon" has a masculine gender:

"the" lemon ⟹ "EL" limón

"the" lemons ⟹ "LOS" limones

♡ **El limón**   ♡ **Los limones**

--- Typical Spanish: food

> ♡ **Desert: Fruit ~**
> **Postre: Fruta**

P	I	Ñ	A	W	L	A
E	L	X	E	Y	I	U
A	U	Á	F	U	V	K
J	K	N	T	A	L	E
N	E	A	S	A	P	U
A	B	Z	H	U	N	W
R	U	N	E	K	B	O
A	S	A	N	D	I	A
N	O	M	L	O	E	Z

> ♡ Please find the food in the word search

Piña ☐   **Manzana** ☐   **Uvas** ☐

Plátano ☐   **Sandia** ☐   **Naranja** ☐

--- Typical Spanish: food

In Spanish to say ...

I like ... we say.... **Me gusta OR Me gusta<u>n</u>**

we say

Me gusta when referring to 1 thing
and
Me gusta<u>n</u> when referring to 2 things or more

♡ **Me gusta la piña**
~ I like pineapple~

♡ **Me gusta<u>n</u> las fresas**
~ I like strawberries~

♡ Can you write in <u>English</u> what she is saying?

♡ **Me gusta el plátano y me gustan las peras.**

--- Typical Spanish: food

♡ Draw a picture of the following items

♡ Una Pera

♡ Un limón

♡ Unas cerezas

♡ Unas uvas

♡ Una sandia

♡ Remember

♡ "a" & "an" = "un" or "una"
♡ "some" = "unos" or "unas"

--- Typical Spanish: food

♡ Deserts ~ Postres

Spanish children's favorite deserts!!!

♡ Natillas	♡ A custard dessert
♡ Flan	♡ A crème caramel
♡ Arroz con leche	♡ Rice pudding
♡ Torrija	♡ Spanish French toast
♡ Helado	♡ Ice cream

♡ Ice creams - Helados

♡ Helado de Vainilla	♡ Vanilla ice cream
♡ Helado de Chocolate	♡ Chocolate ice cream
♡ Helado de limón	♡ Lemon ice cream
♡ Helado de coco	♡ Coconut ice cream
♡ Helado de Fresa	♡ Strawberry ice cream

--- Typical Spanish: food

♡ Can you write in English what the children are ordering?

♡ **Por favor, quiero un helado de vainilla**

♡ **Buenas tardes, un flan y un helado de chocolate por favor**

♡ **Hola, dos helados de limón, un arroz con leche y un flan.**

--- Typical Spanish: food

♡ Match the English with the Spanish words

♡ Arroz con leche

♡ Flan

♡ Spanish French toast

♡ Natillas

♡ Helado de Vainilla

♡ Ice cream

♡ Rice pudding

♡ Helado de Fresa

♡ Vanilla ice cream

♡ Helado

♡ Straberry ice cream

♡ A crème caramel

♡ A custard dessert

♡ Torrija

--- Typical Spanish: food

♡ **Deserts: Ice creams ~ Postres: Helados**

♡ Dos helados de vainilla y uno de chocolate por favor.

Tom

♡ Hola, quiero un helado de coco y un helado de fresa.

William

♡ Tres helados de chocolate, uno de vainilla y uno de limón.

Rose

♡ Buenos tardes, un helado de fresa y una botella de agua fria por favor.

Oliver

♡ Who is ordering what? Can you match the order with the name?

♡ A strawberry ice cream and a cold bottle of water.

♡ Two vanilla ice creams and a chocolate ice cream.

Rose

♡ A coconut and a strawberry ice cream.

Tom

William

♡ Three chocolate ice creams and a coconut and a lemon ice cream.

Oliver

--- Typical Spanish: food

♡ **Sweets:**
Dulces ~ Golosinas

Spanish children's favorite sweets!

♡ Gominolas	♡ Gummies
♡ Regaliz	♡ Liquorice
♡ Caramelos	♡ Sweets
♡ Sugus	♡ Assorted fruit chews
♡ Chupa chups	♡ Lollipop
♡ Pipas	♡ Sunflower seeds
♡ Gusanitos	♡ Corn puffs
♡ Chicle	♡ Chewing gum
♡ Naranjas y limones	♡ Sour gummies
♡ Pictolin	♡ Menthol flavour sweet
♡ Puntazos	♡ A corn snack

--- Typical Spanish: food

♡ **Can you find the 3 odd answers**

♡ **No me gusta el regaliz**

♡ **Me gustan los caramelos y las pipas.**

♡ **Me gustan las gominolas**

- ♡ I like liquorice
- ♡ I don't like lollipops
- ♡ I like chewing gum
- ♡ I like gummies
- ♡ I don't like liquorice
- ♡ I like sweets and sunflower seeds

♡ **Can you write in <u>Spanish</u> what she is saying?**

♡ **Pipas y un chupa chups por favor.**

- -

--- Typical Spanish: food

♡ Please find the sweets in the word search below

Regaliz ☐

Chicle ☐

Pipas ☐

Sugus ☐

Gusanitos ☐

N	S	V	I	A	P	B	O	I
M	O	U	C	H	I	C	L	E
K	A	B	G	C	P	U	Q	A
U	L	E	O	U	A	D	J	U
Q	K	R	B	U	S	I	V	Z
E	Z	I	L	A	G	E	R	I
G	U	S	A	N	I	T	O	S

♡ Can you write in <u>Spanish</u> what sweets do you like?

- -

- -

--- Typical Spanish: food

♡ Fill in the blanks

♡ S _ _ US   ♡ _ _ _ ALI_

♡ C_ _ _ _ E   ♡ _ O _ I _OLA _

♡ PU _ _ A _ _ _   ♡ _ _ SA _ I _ O_

♡ How do you name these in Spanish?

- - - - - - - - - - - - - - - - -

- - - - - - - - - - - - - - - - -

- - - - - - - - - - - - - - - - -

- - - - - - - - - - - - - - - - -

--- Places to visit ---

 ## In Spanish to say ...

 ♡ **The bakery** ♡ **La panadería**
we say

 ♡ **The fruit shop** ♡ **La frutería**
we say

 ♡ **The sweet shop**
we say ♡ **La tienda de golosinas**

 ♡ **The supermarket**
♡ **El supermercado**
we say

 ♡ **The restaurant**
♡ **El restaurante**
we say

 ♡ **The cinema** ♡ **El cine**
we say

--- Places to visit ---

 In Spanish to say ...

♡ The train / bus station
we say
♡ La estación de tren / autobús

♡ The library ♡ La biblioteca
we say

♡ The hotel
we say ♡ El hotel

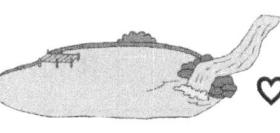
♡ The swimming pool
we say ♡ La piscina

♡ The park ♡ El parque
we say

--- Places to visit ---

♡ **Can you find the words below in Spanish?**

♡ Cinema   ♡ Bakery   ♡ Shop

♡ Swimming pool   ♡ Fruit shop   ♡ Hotel

♡ Park   ♡ Library

--- Places to visit ---

♡ Match the English with the Spanish words

♡ Piscina

♡ Fruit shop

♡ Biblioteca

♡ Bakery

♡ Sweet shop

♡ Cine

♡ Library

♡ Tienda de golosinas

♡ Train station

♡ Cinema

♡ Swimming pool

♡ Estación de tren

♡ Panadería

♡ Frutería

--- At the beach ---

 ## In Spanish to say ...

we say

♡ The beach	♡ La playa
♡ The sea	♡ El mar
♡ The sand	♡ La arena
♡ The sun	♡ El sol
♡ The parasol	♡ La sombrilla
♡ The float	♡ El flotador
♡ The toilets *for women *for men	♡ Los servicios / aseos * para mujeres * para hombres
♡ The showers	♡ Las duchas
♡ The cafe	♡ El café
♡ The beach bar	♡ El chiringuito
♡ The table	♡ La mesa
♡ The chair	♡ La silla
♡ The bill	♡ La cuenta

--- Places to visit ---

In Spanish to say ...

Where is ... ?   Where are ... ?
  we say   we say
¿Dónde está ...?   ¿Dónde est<u>á</u>n ...?

♡ ¿Dónde está la playa?

~ Where is the beach? ~

♡ ¿Dónde est<u>á</u>n los servicios?

~ Where are the toilets? ~

♡ Can you write in <u>English</u> what she is saying?

♡ ¿Dónde está el chiringito?

♡ ¿Dónde están las mesas?

--- Places to visit ---

♡ Match the English with the Spanish words

♡ ¿Dónde está la tienda de golosinas?

♡ ¿Dónde está la panadería?

♡ ¿Dónde está el supermercado?

♡ ¿Dónde está el sol?

♡ ¿Dónde está el cine?

♡ ¿Dónde está el hotel?

♡ Sweet shop

♡ Bakery

♡ Sun

♡ Cinema

♡ Supermarket

♡ Hotel

--- Places to visit ---

♡ Can you write in <u>English</u> what the children are saying?

♡ ¿Dónde está la frutería?

_____

♡ ¿Dónde está el restaurante?

_____

♡ Can you write in <u>Spanish</u> what is she saying?

♡ Hello, where is the sweet shop?

_____

--- In the restaurant ---

Imagine you are in a Restaurant ...

♡ Look at the conversation below

♡ **Camarero** **¿Qué vas a tomar?**
(waiter)
~ What are you having ? ~

Quiero un zumo de naranja
~ I want an orange juice ~

♡ **Camarero** **¿Algo más?**
~ Anything else~

Si, quiero una ración de tortilla de patata sin cebolla.
~ Yes, I want a portion of Spanish omelet without onions ~

♡ **Camarero** **¿Algo más?**
~ Anything else~

No gracias
~ No thank you ~

  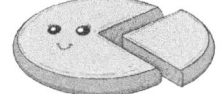

--- In the restaurant ---

Imagine you are in a Restaurant ...

♡ Look at the conversation below

♡ **Camarera** (waitress) **Buenas tardes ¿Qué vas a tomar?**

~ Good afternoon, what are you having? ~

¿Hay batido de fresa?

~ Is there strawberry milkshake? ~

♡ **Camarera**

No lo siento,
¿Quieres batido de chocolate?

~ No, I'm sorry, do you want a chocolate milkshake? ~

Si por favor, un batido de chocolate y paella de pollo.

~ Yes please, a chocolate milkshake and chicken paella ~

♡ **Camarera** **¿Algo más?**

~ Anything else? ~

No gracias

~ No thank you ~

-- Ice cream parlour --

Imagine you are in an ice cream parlour ...

♡ Look at the conversation below

♡ **Camarero** **Buenos días, ¿Qué vas a tomar?**
~ Good morning, what are you having? ~

Hola, Quiero un helado de vainilla
~ Hello, I want a vanilla ice cream ~

♡ **Camarero** **¿Algo más?**

~ Anything else ? ~
No gracias, ¿Cuánto es?
~ No thank you, how much is it? ~

♡ **Camarero** **Son dos euros**

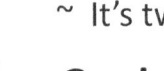
~ It's two euros ~

Gracias, adiós
~ Thank you, bye ~

Helados

--- Sweet shop ---

Imagine you are in an Spanish sweet shop ...

♡ **Look at the conversation below**

♡ **Dependienta**
(shop assistant)

Hola, ¿Qué quieres?
~ Hello, what do you want? ~

Hola, Quiero un chupa chups y regaliz
~ Hello, I want a lollipop and liquorice ~

♡ **Dependienta**

¿Algo más?
~ Anything else ? ~

No, nada más, ¿Cuánto cuesta?
~ No, nothing else, how much is it? ~

♡ **Dependienta**

Es un euro
~ It's a euro ~

Gracias, adiós
~ Thank you, bye ~

Dulces ~ Golosinas

--- The best questions to ask

 In Spanish to say ...   *we say*

♡ What's your name?	♡ ¿Cómo te llamas?
♡ How are you	♡ ¿Cómo estás?
♡ Is there Paella?	♡ ¿Hay paella?
♡ Are there strawberries?	♡ ¿Hay fresas?
♡ How much is ... the ice cream?	♡ ¿Cuánto es el helado?
♡ How much is ... the water?	♡ ¿Cuánto cuesta el agua?
♡ Where is the swimming pool?	♡ ¿Dónde está la piscina?
♡ Anything else?	♡ ¿Algo más?

--- Spain ---

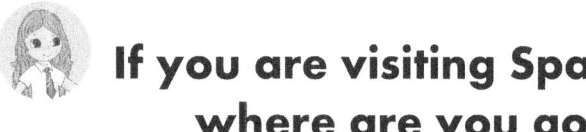

Santiago de Compostela

Barcelona

Madrid

Valencia

Palma de Mallorca

Sevilla

Málaga

If you are visiting Spain soon, where are you going?

_____ ☐   _____ ☐

_____ ☐   _____ ☐

--- Spanish cities ---

 **Most famous cities in Spain.**

Tick the cities you have been before:

- Barcelona ☐
- Madrid ☐
- Valencia ☐
- Málaga ☐
- Pamplona ☐
- Mallorca ☐
- Santiago de Compostela ☐

Which cities would you like to visit?

_____ ☐   _____ ☐

_____ ☐   _____ ☐

--- Madrid ---

Best places to visit

1. **Plaza Mayor** ✓

2. **Puerta del Sol**

3. **Parque del Retiro**

4. **El Museo del Prado**

5. **Parque de atracciones de Madrid**

6. **Estadio Santiago Bernabeu**

7. **El Teleférico**

8. **Sweet Space**

--- Madrid ---

Madrid, the Spanish capital, is a friendly, buzzing city. A fantastic place to explore full of spacious squares, fantastic parks with an excellent metro system, and churros!!!

You will love:

 Weaving through the stone archways at **Plaza Mayor**.

 Spotting the big bear statue in the square **la Puerta del Sol**.

 Walking, cycling OR canoeing in **Parque del Retiro**, Madrid's most famous park.

 Admiring the works by Goya, Velázquez and other Spanish masters in **El Museo del Prado**.

--- Madrid ---

Discovering the magic of the **Parque de Atracciones** de Madrid, enjoy exciting rides and shows.

Visiting **El estadio Santiago Bernabeu**, home of Spanish football club Real Madrid!

Seeing Madrid from a bird's eye view, after taking the cable car **El Teleférico.**

Immersing yourself in **Sweet Space** a candy museum where you'll discover a world of pure imagination.

In my opinion the BEST place is?

_____

_____

Have fun... in Barcelona!

Barcelona

--- Barcelona ---

Best places to visit

1. Park Güell
2. Museo del chocolate
3. Estadio Camp-Nou
4. L'Aquàrium de Barcelona
5. Fuente mágica de Montjüic
6. Casa Batló
7. Cosmocaixa
8. Parque de atracciones Tibidabo

--- Barcelona ---

 Barcelona a city overlooking the Mediterranean Sea, famous for Gaudí's fantastic architecture. A family-friendly destination, where the locals love kids, and families are made to feel welcome!

You will love:

 Being mesmerized by **Park Güell**, a magical park with AMAZING buildings, sculptures designed by Gaudí

 The **Museo del chocolate**, learning the history of chocolate and taking part in tasting workshops... Yummy!

 Visiting **El estadio Camp-Nou**, home of Spanish football club Barcelona.

 Having fun at **L'Aquàrium de Barcelona**, the biggest aquarium in Europe!

-- Barcelona --

 Enjoying **Montjuïc la Fuente mágica**, a spectacular display of light, music and water acrobatics!

 Seeing **Casa Batló**, Gaudí's magical house, an icon in Barcelona.

 Discovering **Cosmocaixa**, a museum designed for children dedicated to everything related to Science!

 Having fun in **Tibidabo** amusement park, including the fun getting there by the **Tibidabo Funicular**.

 In my opinion the BEST place is?

_____

_____

--- Valencia ---

Best places to visit

- La ciudad de las artes y las ciencias ☐
- Parque Gulliver ☐
- El Oceanografíc ☐
- Bioparc ☐
- Paseo en barco por la Albufera ☐
- El museo de los Soldaditos de Plomo ☐
- El paseo marítimo ☐

--- Valencia ---

Valencia, a place full of contrasts, with a charming old town next to futuristic buildings!

You will love:

Getting the wow factor at **La ciudad de las artes y las ciencias**, an extremely impressive science complex.

Enjoying **Parque Gulliver** a giganti playground inspired by the classic tale of Gulliver's Travels.

Being transport to the sea world at **El Oceanográfic**, Europe's largest aquarium, housing more than 45,000 marine creatures.

--- Valencia ---

 A stunningly gorgeous zoo, the **Bioparc!** With beautiful and realistic habitats for the animals.

 Immersing yourself in the Albufera Natural Park with a traditional boat ride, **Paseo en barco por la Albufera,** on the large lagoon.

 Admiring **El Museo de Soldaditos de Plomo**, the biggest Toy soldiers Museum in the world.

 Going for a walk to **El Paseo marítimo**, with its stunning views and refreshing sea breeze.

In my opinion the BEST place is?

_____

_____

Have fun... in Sevilla!

--- Sevilla ---

 **Best places to visit**

 **Plaza de España**

 Setas de Sevilla

 **Isla Mágica**

 **Museo de las ilusiones**

 **Espéctaculo flamenco**

 **Crucero por el Guadalquivir**

--- Sevilla ---

Seville is a very child friendly, lively city with lots of atmosphere in its streets, famous for its music and flamenco dancing!

You will love:

Seeing the **Plaza de España**, a very impressive semi-circular building with spectacular views and with horse carriages, boat rides and entertainers.

Visiting the spectacular **Setas de Seville,** the largest wooden structure in the world ... using virtual reality to peer into the Roman past.

Traveling in time in The **Isla Mágica** theme park 6 theme areas and discover, the 16th and 17th centuries.

--- Sevilla ---

Entering the fascinating world of illusions in the **Museo de las ilusiones** which will trick your confidence in senses; a world that will confuse you completely, but also educate you...

Visiting a **Espectáculo Flamenco** a unique space, where music, dance and song come together to make you feel the emotion of flamenco within you.

Embarking on a journey along the Guadalquivir River with a **Crucero**.

In my opinion the BEST place is?

_____

_____

Have fun... in Málaga!

Best places to visit ✓

1. Tivoli parque de atracciones
2. Museo interactivo de la música
3. El museo del aeropuerto

--- Málaga ---

 A city full of passion that anyone would want to explore, **on the shores of the Mediterranean, with a fascinating cultural side.**

You will love:

Visiting **Tivoli** amusement park with incredible shows and more than 40 attractions, a great destination!

The **Museo Interactivo de la Mùsica**, for an exciting day of experimenting and learning about different instruments.

El Museo del aeropuerto getting a look inside the cockpit and compare the pilot uniforms of the past to the ones you see today.

In my opinion the BEST place is?

_____
_____

Have fun... in Mallorca!

Best places to visit ✅

- Ferrocarril de Sóller
- Rancho grande
- Alcudia

-- Palma de Mallorca --

Mallorca is one giant adventure playground, a paradise for kids and there is always something new to experience and enjoy.

You will love:

To hop onto the **Ferrocarril de Sòller** to experience the beauty of the island on the famous vintage wooden train.

Getting ready to feel like a cowboy as you enter into the El **Rancho Grande**.

Alcudia a paradise for stand-up paddling, take this activity to a new level on the island.

In my opinion the BEST place is?

--- Santiago ---

Santiago de Compostela is small and picturesque, like a fairy-tale city. It is also quiet, safe and very pleasant to stroll through

Santiago

You will love:

Visiting the famous **Catedral**

The **Mercado de Abastos,** the famous food market.

Walking the last few Kilometers of the **Camino De Santiago**, easy to follow as there are plenty of "scallop signs" indicating the path and a lot of pilgrims walking everywhere!

In my opinion the BEST place is?

_____

_____

Ready to go... on holidays?

Let's put in practice what we have learned

14 tasks

160 Challenges

250 points to earn ...

Are you up to the challenge??

--- Fun Tasks ---

How does it work ...

You are awesome and you should be very proud of yourself!

You have learned so many new words in Spanish and you are ready to put them in to practice in Spain!

This part of the book is full of fun tasks to do in Spain. Every time you complete a task tick a box. You must tick all the boxes to complete the challenges!
No cheating!!!

♡ Congratulations!

 ♡ Some tasks have DOUBLE or TRIPLE points as they are more challenging

Fun tasks

♡ Each task asks you to write in Spanish what you need to say. Example:

Hello in Spanish

Hola

- - - - - - - - - - - - - -

--- Fun Tasks ---

♡ During your holidays say in Spanish, at least 6 times:

Fun task 1 ✅

Hello

Hola

Good morning

Good afternoon

Good evening

♡ Total ___ / 24

--- Fun Tasks ---

♡ During your holidays say in Spanish, at least 6 times:

Fun task 2 ✅

Thank you

- - - - - - - - - - - - - - -

You welcome

- - - - - - - - - - - - - - -

Please

- - - - - - - - - - - - - - -

Yes

- - - - - - - - - - - - - - -

♡ Total ____ / 24

--- Fun Tasks ---

♡ During your holidays say in Spanish, at least 6 times:

Fun task 3 ✅

How are you?

Very well

Goodbye

See you later

♡ Total ___ / 24

--- Fun Tasks ---

♡ During your holidays say in Spanish, at least 6 times:

n task 4 ✓

Water

Milk shake

Juice

Bottle

♡ Total ___ / 24

--- Fun Tasks ---

♡ During your holidays say in Spanish, at least 10 times:

Fun task

⭐ **Order a drink** ⭐

What did you ask for each time?

Example: Un zumo de naranja por favor

✏️ _____   ✏️ _____

✏️ _____   ✏️ _____

✏️ _____   ✏️ _____

✏️ _____   ✏️ _____

✏️ _____   ✏️ _____

♡ ♡ ♡ ♡ ♡
 ♡ ♡ ♡ ♡
      ♡

♡ Total ___ / 20

--- Fun Tasks ---

♡ During your holidays say in Spanish, at least 5 times:

Fun task 6

Order breakfast
What did you ask for each time?

Example: Tostadas y un vaso de leche

_____

_____

_____

_____

_____

♡ Total ___ / 10

--- Fun Tasks ---

♡ During your holidays say in Spanish, at least 8 times:

Fun task 7

 Use "Hay"

Ask if there is / there are a specific drink
What did you ask for each time?
Example: ¿Hay batido de plátano?

_____   _____

_____   _____

 Use "Hay"

Ask if there is / there are a specific fruit
What did you ask for each time?
Example: ¿Hay fresas?

_____   _____

_____   _____

♡ Total ___ / 16

--- Fun Tasks ---

♡ During your holidays say in Spanish, at least 10 times:

Fun task 8

Use "Me gusta / Me gustan"
What did you say each time?

Example: me gusta el helado de vainilla, me gustan los caramelos

♡ Total ___ / 20

--- Fun Tasks ---

♡ During your holidays say in Spanish, at least 5 times:

Fun task 9

Use "Quiero"
**Order a specific MEAL you want
What did you ask for each time?**

Example: Quiero pollo y un vaso de agua por favor

_____

_____

_____

_____

_____

♡ Total ___ / 15

--- Fun Tasks ---

♡ During your holidays say in Spanish, at least 5 times:

Fun task 10

 Use "Quiero"

Order a specific DESSERT you want
What did you ask for each time?

Example: Quiero arroz con leche

_____

_____

_____

_____

_____

♡ Total ___ / 15

--- Fun Tasks ---

♡ During your holidays say in Spanish, at least 3 times each:

Fun task 1

Ask
how much is something?
What did you say each time?

Example: ¿Cuánto es una botella de agua?
¿Cuánto cuesta un chupachus?

_____

_____

_____

Fun task 1

Ask for the bill

Example: La cuenta por favor

♡ Total ___ / 18

--- Fun Tasks ---

♡ During your holidays say in Spanish, at least 4 times:

Fun task 13

Order ice creams
What flavours did you order?

Example: Un helado de coco

_____   _____

_____   _____

☐ ☐ ☐ ☐

Order sweets
What did you order each time?

Example: pipas por favor

_____   _____

_____   _____

☐ ☐ ☐ ☐

♡ Total ___ / 16

--- Fun Tasks ---

♡ During your holidays say in Spanish, at least 2 times:

Fun task 14

Use "¿Dónde está ...?"
Ask where is a specific place
What did you ask for each time?
Example: ¿Dónde está el supermercado?

_____

_____

Use "¿Dónde están ...?"
Ask where are some specific items
What did you ask for each time?
Example: ¿Dónde están los sugus?

_____

_____

♡ Total ___ / 12

--- Fun Tasks ---

♡ During your holidays say in Spanish, at least 3 times:

Fun task 15

White a conversation you have had during your holidays in Spanish! What did you say for each time?

♡ Total ___ / 9

♡ **GRAN Total** ___ / 250

--- Notes ---

--- Vocabulary ---

English	Spanish	English	Spanish
Friends	Amigos	Yes	Si
Brother	Hermano	No	No
Sister	Hermana	And	Y
Hello	Hola	Please	Por favor
I'm called…	Me llamo	Thank you	Gracias
Good morning	Buenos días	You are welcome	De nada
Good afternoon	Buenas tardes	Big	Grande
Good evening	Buenas noches	Small	Pequeño/a
How are you?	¿Cómo estás?	With	Con
Very well	Muy bien	Without	Sin
Thank you	Gracias	One	Uno
See you later	Hasta luego	Two	Dos
Goodbye	Adiós	Three	Tres

--- Vocabulary ---

English	Spanish	English	Spanish
Four	Cuatro	Orange juice	Zumo de naranja
Five	Cinco	Peach juice	Zumo de melocotón
Six	Seis	Lemonade	Limonada
Seven	Siete	Ice	Hielo
Eight	Ocho	Cold	Frio/a
Nine	Nueve	Bottle	Botella
Ten	Diez	Glass	Vaso
Water	Agua	Cereals	Cereales
Sparkling water	Agua con gas	Toast	Tostada
Mineral water	Agua sin gas	Butter	Mantequila
Milk	Leche	Marmalade	Mermelada
Milk shake	Batido	Tomato	Tomate
Juice	Zumo	Bacon	Panceta

--- Vocabulary ---

English	Spanish	English	Spanish
Fried eggs	Huevos fritos	Chicken	Pollo
Churros	Churros	Calamari	Calamares
Yogurt	Yogur	Prawns	Gambas
Fruit	Fruta	Sea food	Marisco
Bread	Pan	Serrano ham	Jamón serrano
Chocolate	Chocolate	Ham	Jamón
Biscuits	Galletas	Loin fillet	Lomo
Tapas	Tapas	Sandwich	Bocadillo
Paella	Paella	Sandwich	Sandwich
Russian salad	Ensalada rusa	Filling	Relleno
Spanish omelette	Tortilla española	Nutella	Nutella
Croquettes	Croquetas	Cheese	Queso
Portion	Ración	Chorizo	Chorizo

--- Vocabulary ---

English	Spanish	English	Spanish
Drink	Bebida	Rice pudding	Arroz con leche
Orange	Naranja	Ice cream	Helado
Apple	Manzana	Coconut	Coco
Banana	Plátano	Vanilla	Vainilla
Strawberries	Fresas	Gummies	Gominolas
Pineapple	Piña	Liquorice	Regaliz
Watermelon	Sandia	Sweets	Caramelos
Cherries	Cerezas	Fruit chews	Sugus
Lemon	Limón	Lollipop	Chupa chups
Grapes	Uvas	Sunflower seeds	Pipas
Pear	Pera	Corn puffs	Gusanitos
Custard	Natillas	Chewing gum	Chicle
Crème caramel	Flan	Corn snack	Puntazos

--- Vocabulary ---

English	Spanish	English	Spanish
Breakfast	Desayuno	The beach	La playa
Food / Lunch	Comida	The sea	El mar
Dinner	Cena	The sand	La arena
Dessert	Postre	The sun	El sol
Tea/ afternoon snack	Merienda	The parasol	La sombrilla
Sweets	Dulces / Gominolas	The float	El flotador
The bakery	La panadería	The toilets	Los servicios / aseos
The shop	La tienda	For women	Para mujeres
The fruit shop	La Frutería	For men	Para hombres
The sweet shop	La tienda de golosinas	The showers	Las duchas
The supermarket	El supermercado	The cafe	El café
The restaurant	El restaurante	The beach bar	El chiringuito
The cinema	El cine	The table	La mesa
The train / bus station	La estación de tren / autobús	The chair	La silla
The library	La biblioteca	The waiter	El camarero
The hotel	El hotel	The waitress	La camarera
The swimming pool	La piscina	The bill	La cuenta

--- Grammar ---
--- Recap ---

		Masculine	Feminine
In Spanish all nouns are defined as masculine or feminine, there are different genders!	"a" "an"	UN "a" tomato "un" tomate	UNA "a" toast "una" tostada
We also have to be careful if we are talking about one thing or more than one!	Some	UNOS "some" tomatoes "unos" tomates	UNAS "some" toast "unas" tostadas
		Masculine	Feminine
	The	EL "the" lemon "el" limón	LA "the" orange "la" naranja
	There is OR there are	HAY "Hay" melón / "Hay" naranjas There is melon / There are oranges	
In Spanish when saying that we like something we need to put "the" before the thing we like. Be careful with the gender and quantity!	I like	ME GUSTA (1) "I like milk" "me gusta" la leche	ME GUST<u>AN</u> (2 +) "I like pears" "Me gustan las peras"
	I want	QUIERO "I want water" "Quiero agua"	
	Where is ...?	¿DÓNDE ESTÁ ...? Where is the cinema? / ¿Dónde está el cine?	
	Where are ...?	¿DÓNDE EST<u>ÁN</u> ...? Where are the toilets? / ¿Dónde están los servicios?	

 # --- Answers ---

> Hola, Me llamo "Lola"

Pag 8

- Buenas tardes → Good afternoon
- Buenos días → Good morning
- Buenas noches → Good evening

Pag 9

- Hello → Hola
- Adiós → Goodbye
- Thank you → Gracias
- Hasta luego → See you later
- Muy bien → Very well
- ¿Cómo estás? → How are you?

Pag 11

--- Answers ---

♡ Good morning
Buenos días

♡ Good evening
Buenas noches

♡ Good afternoon
Buenas tardes

♡ How are you?
¿Cómo estás?

Pag 12

```
P O R   F A V O R
        D
  S A I C A R G
  I     N
  N
    I   E     O
S       D     N
```

Pag 14

♡ Gracias
Thank you

♡ De nada
You are welcome

♡ Por favor
Please

♡ Grande
Big

♡ Small
Pequeño

Pag 15

--- Answers ---

- ♡ Yes
- ♡ Sin
- ♡ Please
- ♡ You welcome
- ♡ Con
- ♡ Por favor
- ♡ Small
- ♡ Thank you
- ♡ Si
- ♡ Grande
- ♡ With
- ♡ No
- ♡ De nada
- ♡ Big
- ♡ Pequeño
- ♡ Without
- ♡ No
- ♡ Gracias

Pag 16

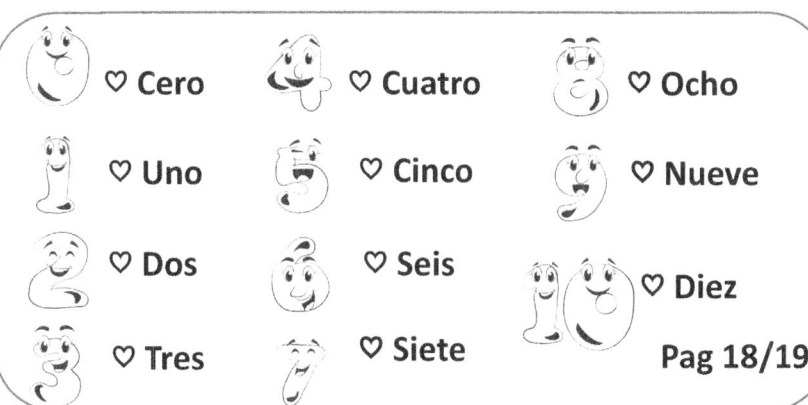

- ♡ Cero
- ♡ Cuatro
- ♡ Ocho
- ♡ Uno
- ♡ Cinco
- ♡ Nueve
- ♡ Dos
- ♡ Seis
- ♡ Diez
- ♡ Tres
- ♡ Siete

Pag 18/19

--- Answers ---

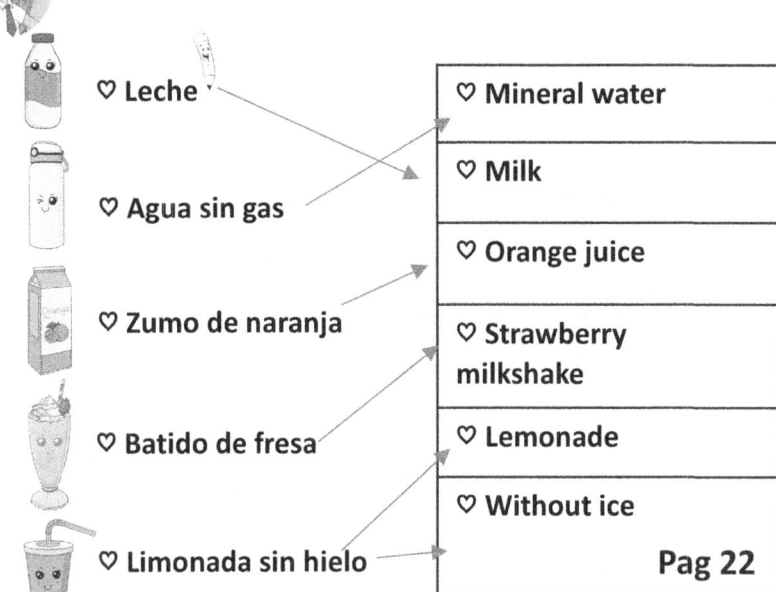

Leche	→	Milk
Agua sin gas	→	Mineral water
Zumo de naranja	→	Orange juice
Batido de fresa	→	Strawberry milkshake
Limonada sin hielo	→	Lemonade / Without ice

Pag 22

♡ Hola, un vaso de leche por favor

Hello, a glass of milk please

♡ Hola, un vaso de limonada por favor

Hello, a glass of lemonade please

Pag 23

A		A			Z	U	M	O
G		J		O				
U		N		L				
A		A		E	E			
		R		I		C		
		A		H			H	
		N						E

Pag 24

--- Answers ---

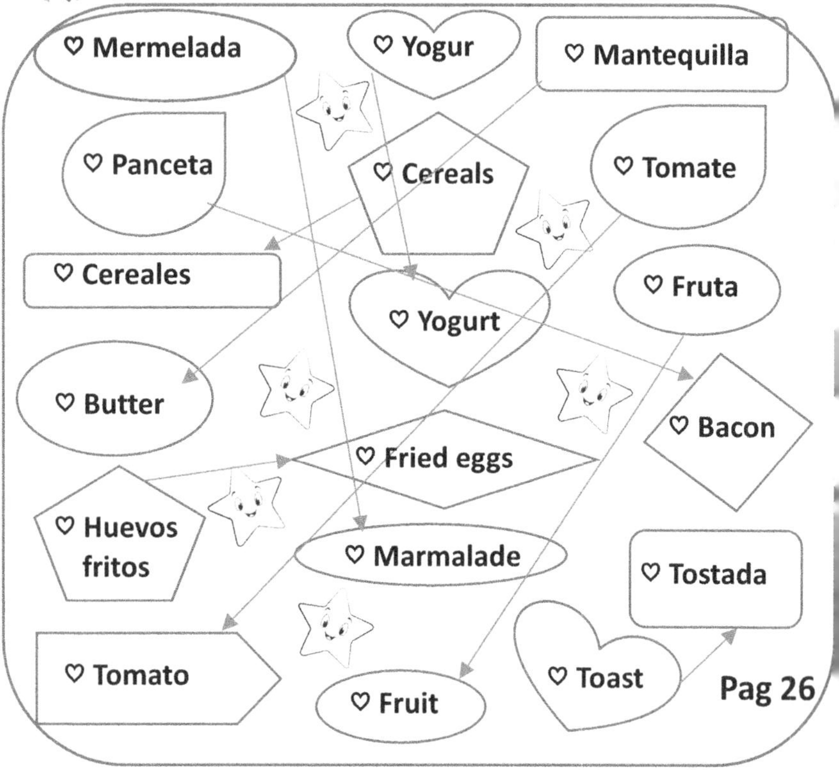

- Mermelada — Marmalade
- Yogur — Yogurt
- Mantequilla — Butter
- Panceta — Bacon
- Cereals — Cereales
- Tomate — Tomato
- Fruta — Fruit
- Huevos fritos — Fried eggs
- Tostada — Toast

Pag 26

♡ **Buenos días, un vaso de leche y unas galletas Maria por favor.**

Good morning, a glass of milk and María biscuits please

♡ **Hola, una tostada con mantequilla, unos churros y un batido de fresa por favor.**

Hello, a toast with butter, some churros and a strawberry milkshake please

Pag 30

♡ **Quiero pan con tomate, unos huevos fritos y panceta, gracias.**

I want bread with tomato, some fried eggs and bacon please

--- Answers ---

♡ **¿Hay yogures?** ~ Are there yogurts~

♡ Si, Hay dos yogures

♡ Si, hay Un yogurt

Pag 31

♡ **Good afternoon, Is there peach juice? I want a peach juice and 2 toasts with butter please**

Good afternoon, ¿Hay zumo de melocotón? Quiero un zumo de melocotón y dos tostadas con mantequilla por favor

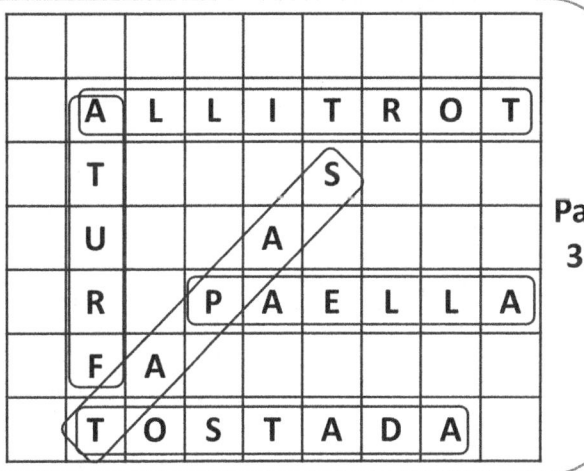

Pag 33

♡ **Hola, una ración de ensalada rusa por favor**

Hello, a portion of Russian salad please

Pag 35

♡ **Buenos días, una ración de croquetas por favor**

Good morning, a portion of croquettes please

--- Answers ---

♡ **Buenos días, quiero una botella de agua por favor**
Buenos días, I want a bottle of water please

♡ **Buenas tardes, una ración de paella y agua sin gas con hielo por favor**
Good afternoon, a portion of paella and mineral water with ice please.

♡ **Hola, quiero un zumo de naranja y una ración de tortilla de patata sin cebolla.**
Hello, I want an orange juice and a portion of Spanish omelette without onion.

Pag 36

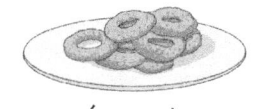

Hay siete calamares

Hay tres

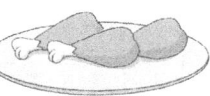

Hay un huevo frito

Pag 3

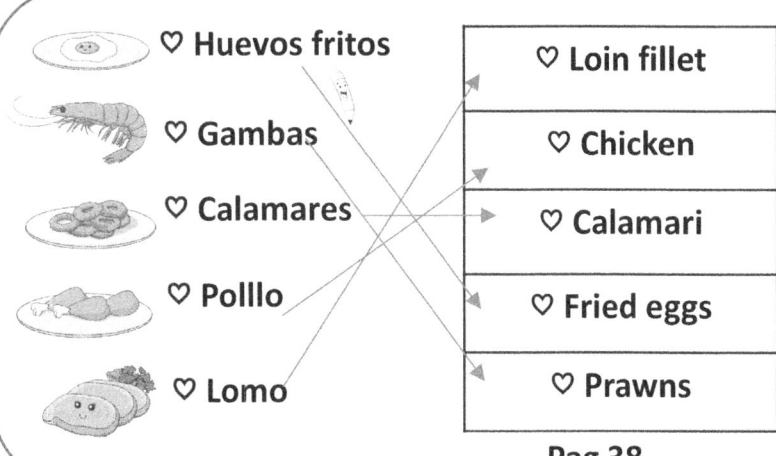

♡ Huevos fritos — ♡ Fried eggs
♡ Gambas — ♡ Prawns
♡ Calamares — ♡ Calamari
♡ Pollo — ♡ Chicken
♡ Lomo — ♡ Loin fillet

Pag 38

--- Answers ---

1 ♡ A serrano ham and a glass of water with ice. → **Alice**

2 ♡ A Nutella sandwich and an orange juice. → **Molly**

3 ♡ A ham sandwich and a bottle of water. → **Noah**

4 ♡ A chorizo and cheese sandwich and a strawberry milkshake. → **Oliver**

Pag 40

♡ **Quiero fresas por favor**
I want strawberries please

Pag 41

P	I	Ñ	A			
	L					U
A		Á		V		
J		N	T	A		
N		A	S	A		
A		Z		N		
R		N				O
A	S	A	N	D	I	A
N		M				

Pag 44

♡ **Me gusta el plátano y me gustan las peras.**
I like banana and I like pears

Pag 45

--- Answers ---

♡ **Por favor, quiero un helado de vainilla**

Please, I want a vanilla ice-cream

♡ **Buenas tardes, un flan y un helado de chocolate por favor**

Good afternoon, a custard and a chocolate ice-cream please.

Pag 48

♡ **Hola, dos helados de limón, un arroz con leche y un flan.**

Hello, two lemon ice-creams, a rice pudding and a custard

- ♡ Arroz con leche
- ♡ Flan
- ♡ Spanish French toast
- ♡ Natillas
- ♡ Helado de Vainilla
- ♡ Ice cream
- ♡ Rice pudding
- ♡ Vanilla ice cream
- ♡ Helado de Fresa
- ♡ Helado
- ♡ A crème caramel
- ♡ A custard dessert
- ♡ Strawberry ice cream
- ♡ Torrija

Pag 49

--- Answers ---

1 ♡ A strawberry ice cream and a cold bottle of water.

Pag 50

2 ♡ Two vanilla ice creams and a chocolate ice cream.

→ *Rose*

3 ♡ A coconut and a strawberry ice cream.

→ *Tom*

→ *William*

4 ♡ Three chocolate ice creams and a coconut and a lemon ice cream.

→ *Oliver*

♡ I like chewing gum   ♡ I don't like lollipops

♡ I like liquorice

♡ **Pipas y un chupa chups por favor**.

Sunflowers seeds and a lollipop please

Pag 52

Pag 53

--- Answers ---

- Me gusta ..... (answers might vary)
- Me gustan ..... (answers might vary)

Pag 53

- ♡ S<u>UG</u>US
- ♡ <u>REG</u> ALI<u>Z</u>
- ♡ C<u>HI</u> <u>CL</u> E
- ♡ <u>G</u>O <u>MI</u><u>N</u>OLA<u>S</u>
- ♡ PU <u>NT</u> A<u>ZOS</u>
- ♡ <u>GU</u> SA <u>N</u> I <u>T</u> O<u>S</u>

- Helado
- Sugus
- Caramelo
- Chupa chus

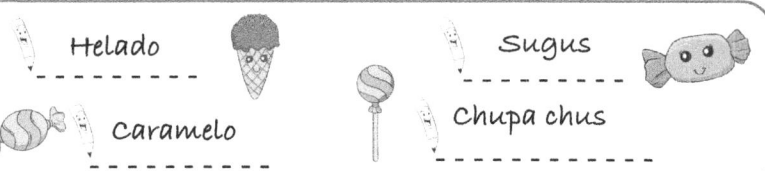

Pag 54

--- Answers ---

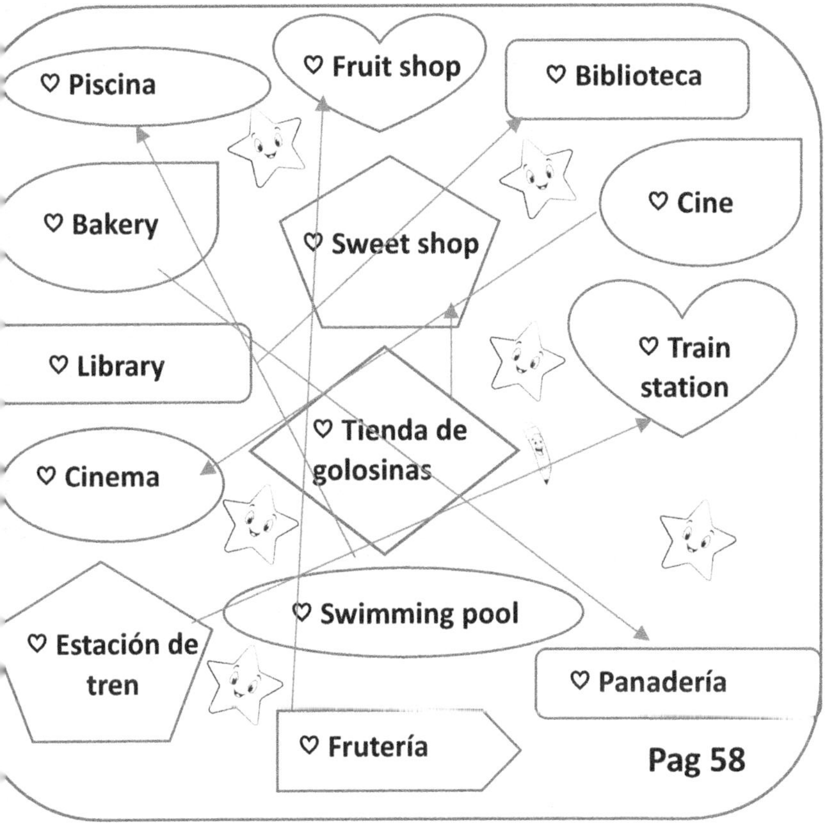

- Piscina → Swimming pool
- Fruit shop → Frutería
- Biblioteca → Library
- Bakery → Panadería
- Sweet shop → Tienda de golosinas
- Cine → Cinema
- Library → Biblioteca
- Train station → Estación de tren
- Cinema → Cine
- Tienda de golosinas → Sweet shop
- Estación de tren → Train station
- Swimming pool → Piscina
- Panadería → Bakery
- Frutería → Fruit shop

Pag 58

♡ ¿Dónde está el chiringito?

Where is the beach bar?

Pag 60

♡ ¿Dónde están las mesas?

Where are the tables?

--- Answers ---

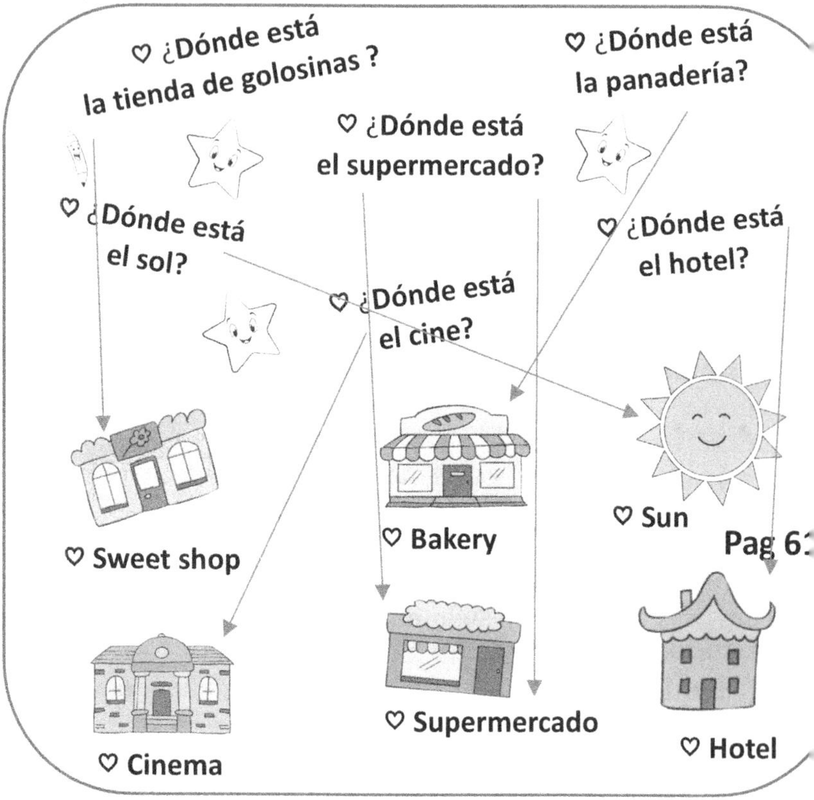

♡ ¿Dónde está la tienda de golosinas? → Sweet shop
♡ ¿Dónde está el supermercado? → Supermercado
♡ ¿Dónde está la panadería? → Bakery
♡ ¿Dónde está el sol? → Sun
♡ ¿Dónde está el cine? → Cinema
♡ ¿Dónde está el hotel? → Hotel

♡ **¿Dónde está la frutería?**
Where is the fruit shop?

♡ **¿Dónde está el restaurante?**
Where is the restaurant?

♡ **Hello, where is the sweet shop?**
Hola, ¿Dónde está la tienda de golosinas?

The End!

See you again soon!

--- Travel Diary ---

m t w t f s s   **Date**: _____

What did you do today?

_____
_____
_____
_____

Weather: ✓

- ☀️ ☐
- ☁️ ☐

The BEST thing about today was?

_____
_____
_____
_____
_____

Today's rating: ⭐ ⭐ ⭐ ⭐ ⭐

--- Travel Diary ---

m t w t f s s   Date: _____

What did you do today?

_____
_____
_____
_____

Weather: ✓

The BEST thing about today was?

_____
_____
_____
_____
_____

Today's rating: ☆ ☆ ☆ ☆ ☆

--- Travel Diary ---

m t w t f s s   **Date:** _____

What did you do today?

_____
_____
_____
_____

Weather: ✓

The BEST thing about today was?

_____
_____
_____
_____
_____

Today's rating: ☆ ☆ ☆ ☆ ☆

♡ FRENCH Available with M...

Age 3+	♡ **My first 100 words... in FRENCH.**
Age 3+	♡ **Dot to dot and colour** while you learn **FRENCH**
Age 4 ~ 8	♡ **Numbers 1 to 10 and Colours** Colour, play and learn **FRENCH** with Mia.
Age 4 ~ 8	♡ **Alphabets and Colours** Colour, play and learn **FRENCH** with Mia.
Age 4 ~ 8	♡ **VOL 1 Colours, Animals, Fruits and Numbers** Colour, play and learn **FRENCH** with Mia

COMING SOON Age 6 +~ **Word searches** for childr...

♡ SPANISH

Age 3+	♡ **My first 100 words... in SPANISH.**
Age 3+	♡ **Dot to dot and colour** while you learn **SPANISH**
Age 4 ~ 8	♡ **Numbers 1 to 10 and Colours** Colour, play and learn **SPANISH** with Mia.
Age 4 ~ 8	♡ **Alphabets and Colours** Colour, play and learn **SPANISH** with Mia.
Age 4 ~ 8	♡ **VOL 1 Colours, Animals, Fruits and Numbers** Colour, play and learn **SPANISH** with Mia
Age 6+	♡ **Word searches** for children ~ **SPANISH** ~
Age 9+	♡ **I am going on holidays to SPAIN!**, the ultimate guide for children to have fun in Spain.

♡ ITALIAN

Age 3+	♡ **Numbers 1 to 10 and Colours**
Age 3+	♡ **Alphabets and Colours**
Age 4 ~ 8	♡ **VOL 1 Colours, Animals, Fruits and Numbers**

Made in the USA
Las Vegas, NV
15 June 2024